S

Computer Tutors

Making Pictures

Anne Rooney

QEB Publishing, Inc.

Published in the United States by
QEB Publishing, Inc.
23062 La Cadena Drive
Laguna Hills, CA 92653

www.qeb-publishing.com

Library of Congress Control Number: 2005921271

ISBN 1-59566-107-7

Written by Anne Rooney
Consultant: Philip Stubbs
Designed by Jacqueline Palmer
Editor: Louisa Somerville
Illustrator: John Haslam
Photographer: Ray Moller
Models provided by Scallywags

Publisher: Steve Evans
Creative Director: Louise Morley
Editorial Manager: Jean Coppendale

Printed and bound in China

Picture credits

The Art Archive /Musée d'Orsay Paris/Dagli Orti (A) 12, /
Museo Lazaro Galdiano Madrid/Joseph Martin 13

Words in bold **like this** are explained in the Glossary on page 30.

Contents

About this book

Lots of things show us copies of the real world—pictures or **models** of real things or people. But we know they aren't really real.

Some things seem more real than others. A movie or TV program looks more real than a black-and-white photo or a cartoon **character**.

A scale model of a car looks more real than a picture of one on a box.

Try it out

Models and pictures have lots of uses. They help us to find out about things and try out ideas. Models help us try things we can't do in real life—or just to have fun.

This book is all about different types of models and pictures on the computer and in the real world.

Making models

On the computer, you can play with models and make pictures, too. You can try out things you can't do in real life—such as driving a car!

Getting dressed

A computer game to dress a baby is a kind of model.

To dress the baby, you use the mouse to drag the clothes to the right parts of the body. It doesn't matter if you get it wrong. It's not like dressing a real baby!

A doll is another kind of model of a baby. It's more like a real baby than the computer game. It's hard to get the arms into the sleeves.

Dressing a real baby is a lot harder! It squirms around. You have to be careful not to hurt the baby.

Have an adventure!

In an adventure game on the computer, you move around in a made-up world.

Make-believe world

In the game, you might have to collect tools, such as magic stones or swords.

You might have to fight monsters or hide from wicked witches.

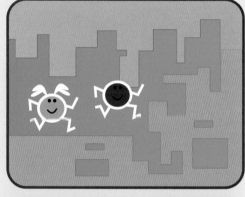

What will I be?

You might have to be a different person or an animal. Maybe you can fly or jump over huge rivers.

Making choices

When you play an adventure game, you choose what to do next.

If other people play, they'll make different choices. Then different things happen.

Models on the computer let us try out different choices.

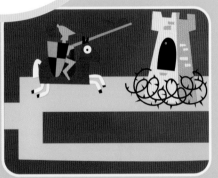

Reality check

How much like real life is a game? The characters don't get tired or need to eat. They don't argue about which way to go.

Looking real

Do you ever get mad if your own pictures don't look "real"? Pictures don't always need to look real!

Getting it right

We all expect pictures to look real in some ways. But we all know they're not real.

Some types of pictures, such as photos, seem more real than others.

It's not real

Even a photo isn't really like a person. It isn't warm to touch. You can't feel the person's clothes or hair.

We know what a cartoon is supposed to be—but it doesn't look very much like the real thing.

What's the difference between a cartoon and a photo?

Practice!

Make a picture of a sheep. How can you make it look more real? Try it out!

Looking at pictures

Pictures don't just show us what things look like. They can show us what the artist thinks or feels about something.

Painting feelings

Some colors can make us feel happy or sad. In this painting, most of the picture is blue, and only the man's face looks real.

The artist used blue to show us that he was feeling sad.

Does the color blue make you feel sad, too?

Which color makes you happy?
Which color makes you sad?
You can use color in your pictures
to show feelings.

Practice!

Use crayons or pens
of different colors
that make you feel
happy and sad.

Painting places

Some pictures aren't
supposed to show us
what something looks
like. They show us
how the artist feels
about the place.

Can you see what this picture shows?
It shows two trees next to a stream.

Paint a picture

You can make your own pictures on paper with crayons, paint, or pens. Or you can make them on the computer with a painting **program**.

Think first!

Think about what you want to paint before you start. Ask some questions:

- What am I trying to do?

- Who will look at my picture?

- How will it be used?

- Should it be big or small?

- How much will I put in?

- Which colors will I use?

Bake Sale
Friday at 3 o'clock

Cat Club
WEB
SITE

In your painting program, choose a paintbrush or a pencil and click on it. Now use the mouse to draw lines.

Look for brushes of different shapes and sizes.

Pick another brush. Experiment. It's not quite like a real painting— it won't smudge, and the colors don't run if you go over a part you've already painted.

Oops!

If you make a mistake, choose Undo to go back a step. That's not quite like a real painting, either!

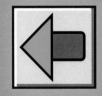

Pick a color

Bold and bright or pale and cool—colors bring your pictures to life.

Paint palette

Your painting program will have boxes of different colors you can pick. To choose a color, just click on it.

Practice!

Draw lines in lots of different colors. What happens if you go over an area you already painted?

Getting warmer...

Different colors have a different "feel."

These are warm colors.

These are cool colors.

These are bright colors.

Spotted patterns

If there's a button for a spray can, you can "spray" spots of paint over your picture.

Practice!

Can you paint cotton candy? Fireworks? A magic wand?

Try spraying one color with the spray can. Then spray another color over the top to mix them.

All shapes

Painting programs make it easy to draw shapes and straight lines.

triangle tool

rectangle/square tool

oval/circle tool

rounded corner box tool

straight line tool

squiggly line tool

Looking for shapes

Find out which shapes you can draw. Can you find out how to draw these?

You can probably draw either filled-in shapes or outlines.

You can choose a color for the filling and a color for the outline. Find out how to do this in your painting program.

Full of color

Find the **flood fill** tool. It might look like a paint can. When you choose this, you can fill a closed area with the color you've chosen.

Coloring it in

Try drawing a pattern or picture with thick black lines on a white background and then fill in the areas with different colors. Can you make a picture like a stained glass window?

Or a painting like the one below?

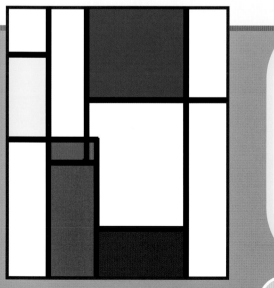

Practice!

Draw a picture from shapes made of black lines on a white screen. Then let a friend color it in.

Do it over!

If you make a mistake, you can use Undo to go back to how your picture was before. But what if you change your mind later on?

You can paint over an area of your picture to change it.

You can also use the eraser to get rid of a part you do not want.

You can change the color of an area with the flood fill tool. Make sure there are no gaps in the outline, or the color will "leak" into the rest of your picture!

It's a good idea to save your picture first. Then you can go back to it if you don't like the changes you make.

Lots of tries!

Save your picture with a different name after you change it. Then you can keep both **versions**.

You can do this to try out different ways of making your picture. Or you can do it to make several pictures that are each a little bit different.

 cat 1

 cat 2

cat 3

Stamp on it!

Using stamps can help to make your picture look more exciting. Stamps put ready-made parts onto your picture for you.

Ready-made pictures

Pick the stamp you want to use and then click where you want it to be on your picture.

There might be different sets of stamps so that you can make different types of pictures.

If you want to make a scene like this, do all the background first. Then use the stamps on top.

Clip art

Another way to add bits is with pictures called **clip art**. They might already be on the computer, or you can get them from a CD-ROM.

It's a lot quicker than drawing everything yourself, but you can still use your imagination.

Finishing up

You might think you're finished—but could you make your picture any better?

Look carefully

When you're done, take a careful look at your picture.

- Is it what you wanted?

- You might want to change the colors, add something, or go over a part you don't like.

Add words

Maybe you could add a **label**. Look for a tool that lets you type words to add to the picture.

Blast off!

Show off!

Show your picture to someone else. They might see how to make it even better.

Save your picture before you change it. Then save it with a new name afterward. You could do three or four and pick the one you like best.

Blast off!

When you're happy with your picture, ask if you can print it out if you want to.

Not all pictures need to be printed. You might make pictures for your school's **website**. People will look at the pictures on a computer.

Over to you

Now it's time to make a picture of your own.

Imagine you can design an outfit for yourself. It might be for a party, or for dressing up to be in a play, or for a sport you like.

Draw a picture of yourself. Choose a paintbrush and draw an outline, or you could use colored shapes. It won't look exactly like you—but it's fun to do! Now save your picture.

Start adding clothes. Use different-shaped tools and brushes to draw t-shirts, pants, skirts, hats, and shoes. Add patterns with a stamp. Use flood fill to try different colors.

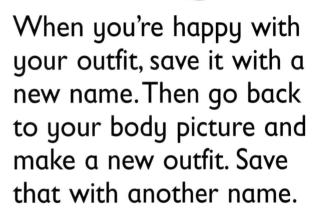

When you're happy with your outfit, save it with a new name. Then go back to your body picture and make a new outfit. Save that with another name.

Make three outfits and then compare them. Which do you like best? Can you make that one any better?

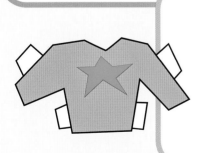

If you print and cut out your body picture and your outfits, you can make a paper doll of yourself. Leave tabs so that you can put the clothes on.

Be a designer

Designers often decorate the things they design to make them look nice.

Your turn

Try drawing a design for something you use. It could be:

- a skateboard

- a bag

- a mug

- a book

or anything else! It's best to choose a simple shape.

The right shape

Start a new picture and draw the outline of the object you have chosen.

Save it with the name "outline."

Pictures or patterns?

Do you want a picture or a pattern? Which colors will you use? Is your design for you or for someone else? Make the design right for the person it's for.

Draw a picture or pattern in the outline and save your work with a new name.

All done!

Check your work, then print it out.

Is it a good design for the object you chose? Could you make it any better?

Glossary

character   Person in a story or adventure game.

clip art   Finished pictures that you can add to your own work on the computer.

flood fill   Tool for filling an area of a picture on the computer with a color.

label   Words added to a picture.

model   Copy of something in the real world.

program   Set of instructions for a computer to follow.

version   One form of something.

website   Set of web pages showing words and pictures that you can see on the World Wide Web.

Index

Grown-up zone

Making Pictures

This book is particularly helpful for supporting children in grades 1 to 3.

It can be used to support computer classes or work on art and design, or it can be tied into class or homework in any other area of the curriculum in which the children use the computer.

Make sure a painting program is set up to make pictures of an appropriate size. Provide stamps that are appropriate for the type of pictures the children are going to make.

Children should have the chance to try out an adventure game on the computer which requires them to make choices or control characters. Get them to discuss the choices they made and the consequences of their choices.

Encourage children to work together and discuss options as they make their pictures. Review their finished work and ask them to talk about why they chose the versions they did, and why they rejected others. Ask them if they can think of any ways of improving their work.

Children should be encouraged to review, evaluate, and improve their own work at all stages. If possible, show them work done by older children and help them to see how this fulfills the same aims that they have in their own work.